SALISBURY

A Brief History

1075–92
Norman cathedral built at Old Sarum.
c.1125
Norman cathedral rebuilt and enlarged.

1220
Bishop Poore lays the foundation stone of the new cathedral.
1227
Henry III grants the first royal charter of liberties to Salisbury.

1258
Consecration of cathedral nave, choir and transepts.
1306
William Russel's house built, possibly the oldest in Salisbury.

c.1315
Completion of cathedral tower and spire.
1331
Cathedral at Old Sarum demolished. Stones used to build Close wall.

c.AD160
Roman fortress – Sarum – established on site of Iron Age town.
c.552
Britons and Saxons battle for Sarum.

1219
Bishop Richard Poore obtains permission to rebuild Salisbury in valley below Old Sarum.

c.1231
St Nicholas's Hospital enlarged by Bishop Bingham to care for poor and sick men and women.
1244
Harnham Bridge built by Bishop Bingham.

1386
The oldest existing clock in England made for the cathedral bell tower.
1483
Duke of Buckingham beheaded in Blue Boar Inn.

Salisbury is unique amongst medieval English cathedral cities. Unlike Winchester or Canterbury or Chester, which grew in higgledy-piggledy fashion from Roman beginnings, Salisbury was methodically laid out in the 13th century, with the cathedral set in its spacious Close nestling in a curve on the River Avon, and the city flowing away to the north in its distinctive 'chequer' pattern.

But the Salisbury of today is the second city to bear that name. The original settlement, known as Sarum, stood on a steep and windswept hill a mile away. A natural stronghold, fortified in prehistoric times, it became the focus for a Roman road network. The Saxons fortified it further, and the later Saxon kings had a mint there; but it was under Norman rule that the fortress flourished, and the foundations of the great castle and cathedral are still visible.

Yet life on the hill was unsettled, with endless clashes between the clergy and the royal garrison; and in 1219, Bishop Richard Poore gained permission from both king and pope to abandon 'Sarisberie', the 'waterless hill fort', and start afresh in the valley below.

1612
James I lodges at the King's House.
c.1660
Beginning of Salisbury's architectural 'golden age'.

1710
Handel gives first public concert in England in room over St Ann's Gate.
1788–91
Restoration of cathedral by James Wyatt.

1714
Completion of the Choristers' School, attributed to Sir Christopher Wren.

1795
The Guildhall donated by the Earl of Radnor.
1860–78
Restoration of cathedral by Sir George Gilbert Scott.

c.1540
Old Sarum totally abandoned.
1611
Salisbury granted charter of incorporation.

1682
Bishop Seth Ward founds College of Matrons.
1665
Charles II stays at Malmesbury House to escape plague.

1668
Samuel Pepys lodges at the Old George Hotel.
1689
James II stays at the Bishop's Palace shortly before his exile to the continent.

1861
Salisbury Museum opens to exhibit the 'Drainage Collection'.
1985
£6,000,000 Spire Appeal launched.

The Cathedral

Salisbury Cathedral is unusual in that it was built 'of a piece' in one architectural style, to the original design of Bishop Poore, and, with the exception of the west front, under the supervision of one man, the master mason Nicholas of Ely. Work was carried out without a break between 1220 and 1266, the only major later additions being the tower and spire, completed in the early 14th century and now a familiar and well-loved landmark. Constructed of Jurassic limestone, a white stone quarried locally, with pillars of dark 'marble' from the Isle of Purbeck in Dorset, the cathedral is a fine example of Early English Gothic style, stunning in its size and simplicity.

The north porch, a painting by J.M.W. Turner

A panel representing fish, a Christian symbol

THE TRINITY CHAPEL

Building of the cathedral began at the east end with the Chapel of the Holy Trinity and All Saints. The chapel is visually remarkable, its roof formed of sharply pointed arches supported on slender pillars of Purbeck marble. A plain Purbeck stone commemorates Osmund, bishop of the first of two Norman cathedrals built at Old Sarum (▷ 3), who was canonized in 1457. The east window, dedicated to prisoners of conscience, offers its rich colours to the rising sun. It was designed and made by Gabriel Loire of Chartres and installed in 1980.

THE QUIRE

At the heart of the cathedral is the quire which, unusually, is not separated from the nave by a screen. Here the bishop has his throne and the clergy and lay canons their stalls, and from here prayer and worship are offered daily to God. Wonderful carvings – birds, animals and foliage – are to be found in the woodwork. Beyond the quire, in the sanctuary, stands the high altar, draped in a frontal portraying Jesus' crown of thorns.

A stained-glass window in the Morning Chapel

The Cathedral

THE CHAPTER HOUSE

The Chapter House dates from the mid 13th century. Octagonal in shape, with a single central pillar from which radiates the delicate fan vaulting, its walls are lined with stone seating for meetings of the 'Chapter', the governing body of the cathedral. Above that is a delightful carved frieze illustrating biblical stories; other carvings depict the vices being trampled by virtues, and the figure of Christ enthroned in majesty. In the Chapter House can be found one of the cathedral's treasures – a copy of the Magna Carta, one of only four in the country.

THE BISHOP'S PALACE

The west wing of the sprawling Bishop's Palace dates from the time of Bishop Poore; later additions were made in the 15th century and in the 17th century, and finally at the end of the 18th century. Today the palace is a gracious setting for pupils of the Cathedral School, and, behind, the wide open spaces of the Close make perfect playing fields.

The Chapter House fan vaulting

The cathedral from the Bishop's Palace, a painting by John Constable

The Chapter House frieze

ENGLAND'S OLDEST CLOCK

The Salisbury Cathedral clock is the oldest surviving in England. Made in 1386, it was originally housed in a separate bell tower, demolished during Wyatt's restoration in 1790. It is driven by a falling weight and strikes the hours, but has no dial or hands.

THE TOWER AND SPIRE

The tower and spire were built about half a century after the rest of the cathedral, and the additional weight caused the four piers at the crossing to bend, so that buttresses and bracing arches were needed for extra support. Further bracing arches were added in the 15th century, in the Perpendicular style. The square tower is topped by an elegant octagonal spire, the tallest in Britain, rising to a height of 123m (404ft) from the ground, and the subject of a recent and much publicized restoration.

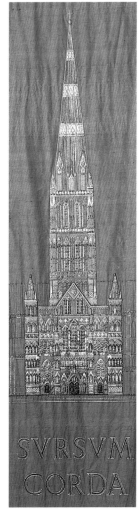

A tapestry of the spire

THE CLOISTER

This naïve but appealing little cat can be found in the cloisters, which are the largest in the country, although Salisbury was never a monastic foundation – they were used instead for processions, and as a quiet spot where the cathedral's canons could relax.

The Close – West Walk

Salisbury's Close is the largest in the country, and the cathedral is surrounded on all sides by vast sweeping lawns, creating a wonderfully pastoral atmosphere. The whole area is protected from the outside world by the comforting bulk of a wall, built in the time of King Edward III using stone from the abandoned cathedral at Old Sarum (▷3). The three sturdy gates to north, east and south are still locked at night.

Beyond the smaller walls that enclose the lawns are 'walks', where the secular canons lived who were responsible for the administration of the cathedral. Today, many of the clergy are more modestly housed elsewhere, and the canonries, many rebuilt, have found new uses, either as private residences – Arundells, Walton Canonry, Myles Place – or as museums.

THE SALISBURY MUSEUM

The Salisbury Museum occupies a house originally built by the medieval Abbots of Sherborne. The stylish alterations carried out in the late 16th and early 17th centuries by Sir Thomas Sadler, Principal Registrar of the diocese, rendered the house fit for a king, and James I was entertained here during several visits to Salisbury. The building was renamed The King's House in his honour. The Museum's exhibitions range from the early history of the area – Stonehenge (▷ 30), Old Sarum (▷ 3) and Salisbury – to collections of photographs, paintings, ceramics and glass, Wedgwood and costume.

The King's House

THE MEDIEVAL HALL

Discreetly hidden behind more modern buildings, but well worth seeking out, lies the 'Medieval Hall' of the Old Deanery, the residence of the Deans of Salisbury Cathedral from the 13th century until 1922. Restored in recent years, the Great Hall of this ancient house, the second to be built in the Close, is a fine example of a medieval banqueting hall. Its magnificent, lofty, trussed rafter roof still survives. A visit to the Hall, now privately owned, is rewarded with a lively and amusing sound and picture show describing Salisbury's history and attractions.

The Medieval Hall

THE WARDROBE

The Wardrobe dates from 1254 and takes its name from its early use as the Bishop's store. It is now the headquarters and museum of the Duke of Edinburgh's Royal Regiment (Berkshire and Wiltshire), the amalgamation in 1959 of two separate regiments formed in the mid 18th century. An extensive and varied collection of the regiment's treasures includes uniform, weapons, medals, paintings and silver. On summer afternoons, tea may be enjoyed in the tranquil garden running down to the river.

The Wardrobe

THE GIANT AND HOB-NOB

Visitors to the Salisbury Museum may be startled to come across the Giant and Hob-nob, a figure 12ft (3.7m) tall accompanied by a hobby horse. The Giant was the pageant figure of the Salisbury Guild of Tailors, and dates at least from 1570. Each year, on midsummer day, the Giant paraded through the streets of Salisbury behind Hob-nob, who caused merriment by chasing and snapping at the on-lookers. More recently this engaging pair, whose appearance has changed many times over the centuries, has emerged only on occasions of national celebration.

The Giant and Hob-nob

BOBBIE OF THE BERKSHIRES

Bobbie, mascot of the 66th (Berkshire) Regiment, was remarkable for surviving a fierce battle between the British and Afghan armies at Maiwand in the hot summer of 1880. The British, defeated, retreated 50 miles across waterless desert – to be joined by a bedraggled Bobbie, believed by all to have been killed. Bobbie became a great favourite of Queen Victoria, who presented him with the Afghan medal seen here – but he met an unfortunate end when he was killed by a runaway hansom cab.

A Salisbury 'kettle', bearing the merchant mark of John Halle

The Close – North Walk

Many of the buildings on the North Walk have seen a change of use over the centuries. Aula Le Stage, dating from the foundation of the cathedral, ceased to be used as a canonry in 1850. The Theological College, although on the site of the medieval School of Theology, was built in the 17th century by a lawyer as his home. Bishop John Wordsworth founded a grammar school in 1890 in a house built by Thomas Chaffyn, a wealthy Wiltshire merchant, in 1649. The building adjoining St Ann's Gate was also a canonry, but in 1660 was leased to the Harris family, who built the extension inside the Close.

Beyond St Ann's Gate, St Ann's Street stretches away with its own delightful jumble of architectural styles, including the Joiners' Hall – and a stunning view back to the cathedral.

MALMESBURY HOUSE

This gracious Queen Anne house, with its intricate Gothic plasterwork and subtle Wedgwood-coloured walls, was designed by Sir Christopher Wren's master builder as an extension to the original dwelling on the east wall of the Close. Completed in 1704, the house took its present name when the tenant, James Harris IV, became the first Earl of Malmesbury in 1800. Since 1968 the house has been restored to its 18th-century splendour by a private owner, and is now open to the public.

A carved stone from Old Sarum in the Close wall near St Ann's Gate

THE SUNDIAL

The sundial on the wall of Malmesbury House dates from 1749 and records both the time and the date. The somewhat gloomy inscription, 'Life's But a Walking Shadow', is from Shakespeare's 'Macbeth'; but, below, a more reassuring text, from St John's Gospel, reminds us that life is eternal.

ST ANN'S GATE

Opening out onto the eastern chequers, St Ann's Gate is topped by a small room that was once a chapel, and later became the music room in Malmesbury House. The composer Handel (1685–1759) is said to have given his first public concert in England here in 1710; he was certainly a regular visitor to Salisbury and a close friend of James Harris III, who was a great patron of music and the arts and hosted many performances in the music room.

Malmesbury House

St Ann's Gate

A ROYAL VISITOR

Plans to assist King Charles II's escape to France in 1651 were hatched by his supporters in Salisbury, and when the plague broke out in London five years after his restoration to the throne, he returned to the city to avoid infection, staying at Malmesbury House. His coat of arms decorates the wall to the right of St Ann's Gate; from here he observed the anxious citizens, then went down among them to give encouragement.

JOINERS' HALL

Towards the top of St Ann's Street is the guildhall of Salisbury's medieval joiners. The skill of the trade is reflected in the richly carved front, added in the 17th century. The building, owned by The National Trust, is not open to the public.

Joiners' Hall

LIFE'S BUT A WALKING SHADOW

THIS IS LIFE ETERNAL THAT THEY MAY KNOW THEE THE ONLY TRUE GOD, AND JESUS CHRIST, WHOM THOU HAST SENT.
ST JOHN CHAPTER 17 VERSE 3.

The sundial on Malmesbury House

The Close – Choristers' Green

The corner of the Close known as Choristers' Green has long associations with the cathedral's choir – a choir school existed here as early as 1323. In the mid 16th century Braybrooke House became home to the headmaster of the choir school, and is connected to the school room in the adjoining Wren Hall. The choirboys were allowed to play on the green to let off steam – hence the name, which is still in use although the school moved to the Bishop's Palace in 1947. The Master of Choristers now lives in Bishop's Walk.

THE CATHEDRAL CHOIR

From the days of the Norman cathedral at Old Sarum, where Bishop Osmund founded a choir school in 1091, daily worship has been sung by boy choristers and vicars choral. In 1991 the 'boys only' tradition was broken when the first girls' cathedral choir in the country was formed at Salisbury, and now the two choirs share the singing of services, concerts, tours and recordings.

BRAYBROOKE HOUSE AND WREN HALL

Braybrooke House was named after William de Braybrooke, a canon in the early 14th century. Although the house began its link with the choir school in 1559, Wren Hall, which provided a school room and dormitories for the choristers, was not built until 1717. Today, Wren Hall houses the cathedral's educational centre.

Braybrooke House and Wren Hall

MOMPESSON HOUSE

In the early 17th century the Dean and Chapter voiced their objection to the taverns in the Close, and forcibly closed them down. One of these was the Eagle Inn on the north side of Choristers' Green, and the site was later leased to Sir Thomas Mompesson, MP for Salisbury. Mompesson House, a perfect example of Queen Anne architecture, was started by Thomas and completed in 1701 by his grand-son Charles. Elegant both outside and in, the house has been restored by The National Trust in period style with fine furniture, china and glass. The lovely walled garden behind the house is an ideal place to rest.

Mompesson House

TROUBLE AT THE DEANERY

In February 1592, the cathedral organist, John Farrant, had an argument with his wife, a niece of the Dean. When the Dean unwisely tried to intervene, Farrant left the choir at Evensong to challenge him at the Deanery (now known as the Medieval Hall ▷ 8). The Dean refused to see Farrant and, much alarmed, retreated to his bedroom. Farrant followed, wielding a knife, but was unable to gain access – whereupon he returned to the cathedral, and joined the choir in singing the anthem.

High Street Gate

The main entrance to the Close is the High Street Gate, with the Close Constable's house and the Porter's Lodge alongside. Tucked into a niche above the gate on the Close side is a statue of King Edward VII, which replaces earlier statues of James I and Charles II. On the High Street side is Charles II's coat of arms.

COLLEGE OF MATRONS

As a young man, Seth Ward, Bishop of Salisbury from 1667 to 1689, proposed marriage to a lady who turned him down and married, instead, a clergyman in the diocese of Exeter. When the lady was widowed, Ward, who had remained a bachelor, founded the College of Matrons, thereby discreetly providing a home for her amidst other clergy widows from the dioceses of Salisbury and Exeter. The building, possibly designed by Wren, still serves that purpose today.

High Street Gate

MITRE HOUSE

Just beyond High Street Gate, on the corner of High Street and New Street, stands Mitre House, instantly identifiable by the large blue bishop's head-dress painted on the side. The house was the first bishop's residence, before the much grander bishop's palace was built within the Close. Its link with the cathedral remains, however, as by a clause in its lease a robing room must be made available for each new bishop on his enthronement.

College of Matrons

THE GOLDEN FLEECE

The figure of a sheep above
No 51 High Street is evidence that
Salisbury's wool trade was briefly
revived in the first half of the
20th century, when the shop was
occupied by a local weaving company,
Stonehenge Woollen Industries.

The Golden Fleece

BEACH'S BOOKSHOP

This well-preserved 14th-century building stands
on a crossroads where once gathered hordes of
clamorous wool traders; but more recently,
it attracted a quieter clientele in its role
as an antiquarian bookshop.

Beach's Bookshop

Festivals and Fun

The whole city – even the cathedral Close, usually so calm and sedate – rises to the occasion with gusto for the many festivals that take place throughout the year – the St George's Day Festival; the summer festival with its variety of events, indoor and outdoor, frivolous and serious, for both young and old; and the colourful Charter Fair, lighting up the Market Square as the October evenings draw in.

ANNUAL FESTIVALS AND EVENTS

Full information is available from the Tourist Information Centre.

April:	St George's Spring Festival
May/June:	Salisbury Festival
June:	Mayor Making Ceremony
	Salisbury Beer Festival
July:	Salisbury Garden and Flower Show
October:	Salisbury Charter Fair
November:	5th Nov. Fireworks Display
December:	Carols by Candlelight
	New Year's Eve Concert in the Medieval Hall

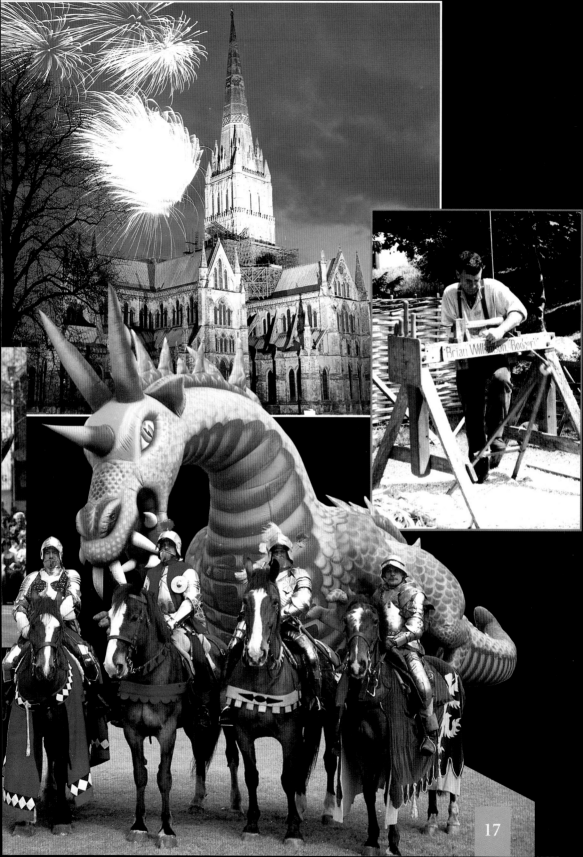

The Water Meadows

The gardens behind the houses on the West Walk of the Close run down to the River Avon, and beyond lie one of Salisbury's delights – the water meadows, which can be enjoyed to the full from the Town Path, leading from Queen Elizabeth Gardens to the medieval Harnham Mill.

HARNHAM MILL

Children and dogs alike love splashing in the river in front of Harnham Mill. Built around 1500 of chequered flint and ashlar, it is thought to have been specially designed for the paper-making industry that flourished in the area between the 16th and 19th centuries; today it provides a serene setting for a restaurant.

CHURCH HOUSE

Lying in a lovely position on the banks of the river is Church House, a private residence until the mid 17th century, when it became what must have been, with its magnificent hall, one of the most stylish of workhouses. In 1881 it was bought and restored by the Church of England, and is now, more fittingly, the headquarters of the Diocese of Salisbury.

Church House

Harnham Mill

JOHN CONSTABLE (1776–1837)

The water meadows were much beloved by the landscape painter John Constable, who spent his honeymoon in Salisbury and was a frequent visitor in the early 19th century, staying at Leadenhall in the Close as a guest of his great friend, Archdeacon John Fisher.

The water meadows in winter

New Street Chequer

The High Street Gate leads away from the peace and tranquillity of the cathedral Close to the immediate hustle and bustle of a thriving market town. Founded by Bishop Poore in 1220, the whole area is laid out on a grid known, descriptively, as 'chequers'.

New Street Chequer takes its name from the ancient street that hugs the northern boundary wall of the Close; to the west of the chequer is the High Street, whilst to the north is New Canal, which was once just that – an open water supply, tapped from the Avon and running down the centre of the street.

JOHN HALLE'S HOUSE

In medieval times, Salisbury's prosperity grew out of its basic commodity – wool, from the sheep that grazed on the surrounding plain. The wealthiest citizens were thus the wool-merchants and later, when England began to make fine cloth instead of exporting the raw material, the clothiers. One such merchant was a somewhat turbulent character, John Halle, also mayor and MP for the city, who built a splendid house in New Canal. John Halle's 'Hall' was restored in 1834 by the Gothic revivalist Pugin, and survives today as the most unusual cinema foyer in the country.

A painting by Louise Rayner of the High Street in c.1870

THE HIGH STREET

The High Street was the main street, linking the Close with the trading area of the city. Halfway along, the Old George Hotel played host to many important visitors, including a troop of Shakespeare's actors who performed 'As You Like It' at nearby Wilton House (▷ 30), and Samuel Pepys, who stayed there in 1668 and found the bill 'exorbitant'. The ground floor has now all but disappeared to give access to a modern shopping mall, but some of the original timbers, as well as the first floor, still remain.

The Old George Hotel

n Halle's Hall and merchant mark

THE NEW INN

Not very new, this inn on New Street dates from the late 15th/early 16th century. It will be appreciated both by non-smokers (since smoking is banned here) and by lovers of fresh air – the pretty garden backs onto those of the cathedral North Walk (▷10), creating a country atmosphere in the midst of the city.

The garden of the New Inn

THE ASSEMBLY ROOMS

The bookshop on the corner of the High Street and New Canal is housed in the city's old Assembly Rooms, and some of the original plasterwork, now restored, can be seen upstairs. Perched on the roof is a witty clock tower, with W H SMITH & SON instead of numerals, after an earlier occupant, and a weathervane in the form of a newspaper boy.

The W H Smith clock and weathervane

THE VENICE OF ENGLAND

Open water channels once flowed through the centre of Salisbury's streets, providing both a water supply and drainage, and inspiring such diverse descriptions as 'pleasant little rivoletts … gliding sweetly' and '… always dirty, full of wet and filth, and weeds'. By 1734, the channels were in a 'sad nasty pickle' and soon after they were moved to one side of the street and laid in brick beds.
The benefits of completely enclosing the water channels in the 1850s were twofold, for not only did the citizens enjoy a much healthier environment, but the myriad objects that were recovered during the works, and dubbed the 'Drainage Collection', became the first exhibit of the highly acclaimed Salisbury Museum (▷8).

The Market Square

When the layout of the town was being planned, a huge chequer was left open as a site for the market. In 1227, a charter granted by Henry III made Salisbury a free city. The chief citizens promptly formed a merchant guild, which became the city's governing body until its formal incorporation in 1611, and the market became a weekly event to provide the basic essentials to a townspeople determined to prosper. An annual fair, dating from the same charter, is still held in October.

The Guildhall

LITTLE TREATS IN SALISBURY

- Afternoon tea at Snell's Tea Rooms (▷28)
- The tranquil garden of Mompesson House (▷13)
- Evensong in the cathedral (▷4–7)
- The enticing aroma of Culpeper's Herbalist
- A stroll through the water meadows (▷18–19)
- A visit to Fisherton Mill – including lunch! (▷24)

THE GUILDHALL

The Guildhall stands at the south-eastern corner of the Market Square, and has always been the commercial heart of the city. Built and rebuilt over the centuries, the present imposing Guildhall was completed in 1795, the gift of the Earl of Radnor. The New Council House, as it was then known, replaced an older Town House, which was severely damaged by fire in 1780. A later addition to the building was a Victorian cell block, tacked on to the west elevation in place of the grand portico seen in the aquatint above. Today, courts are conducted in the Guildhall, and banquets held in an elegant ground-floor room.

The annual charter fair

THE MARKET

Nowadays, the market is held
twice a week. Each Tuesday and
Saturday, Salisbury comes alive
with crowds of people thronging
around the colourful stalls, buying
much the same produce as they
might have at a medieval market –
fruit, vegetables, meat, fish,
flowers and household goods.

BUCKINGHAM'S GHOST

Debenham's department store
stands on the site of a medieval inn,
the Blue Boar, dating from 1455. On
2 November 1483 the Duke of
Buckingham, aged 29, was executed
in the courtyard of the inn following a disagreement with King
Richard III. The Duke vowed to
haunt the inn forever – and sure
enough, each year, on the anniver-
sary of his death, his spirit walks
amongst the merchandise!

The Maltings and Fisherton Street

To the west of the market, on the far side of the river, is a new shopping development known as The Maltings, with the city's cultural centres, the Playhouse and City Hall, beyond. Fisherton Street, lined with eclectic shops and restaurants, grew with the opening of the railway station, and many buildings still retain their Victorian frontages. At the city end of the street, the old hospital has been spared demolition because its architect was the renowned John Wood of Bath, and has now been converted into elegant apartments.

Fisherton Mill

FISHERTON MILL

Although visitors to Fisherton Mill will be distracted by the wonderful collection of multicultural crafts and furniture, a close look at the building itself reveals the lovely weathered features of the original grain mill, dating from 1880. Constantly changing exhibitions are held both inside the mill and in the courtyard outside, and the Gallery Café is very welcoming.

The Maltings

BISHOP'S MILL

The oldest building in The Maltings is the Bishop's Mill, dating from 1757, and so named because it is thought to occupy the site of a mill built by Bishop Richard Poore in the 13th century. Used successively as a grist mill for flour, tobacco and snuff, a fulling mill for cloth, and malthouses for beer and whisky, Bishop's Mill is now a restaurant.

THE GAOL AND CLOCK TOWER

Two walls survive of the old gaol which stood on the west bank of the Avon until the mid 19th century. Before 1835, the city boundary was marked by the river flowing beneath the tiny iron-barred windows. A carving of shackles is a reminder of the building's earlier use; today, it forms the base for a clock tower, added in 1890.

THE MALTINGS

Newly built alongside the river, The Maltings is linked to the city centre by a bridge marking the route by which the shortest standard-gauge railway in the country once ran, bringing produce from the main-line station at the end of Fisherton Street to the market place.

THE MILL RACE

The mill race rushes along noisily at mesmeric speed, yet seems to form an oasis of tranquillity in its busy surroundings.

The Eastern Chequers

Running down the spine of the city is a long thoroughfare, starting with a section named, intriguingly, 'Endless Street', then trailing off rather more conventionally into Queen Street, Catherine Street, St John's Street... To the east of this lies the bulk of the city 'chequers', named after important local merchants – Swayne's, Vanner's, Gore's – or after inns – Cross Keys, Three Cups, Black Horse –, for the construction of a city and the business of making money is thirsty work, and Salisbury has always been well endowed with taverns. Divided by streets of little houses built through the centuries, this is where specialist shops, full of unusual treasures, are to be found.

WILLIAM RUSSEL'S HOUSE

The late 18th-century façade of the building adjoining John a'Port's conceals a remarkably well-preserved house dating from 1306. On the first floor, parts of the original structure have been exposed. This timber window, with wattle and daub infilling, shows how the walls were first constructed.

JOHN A'PORT'S HOUSE

Opposite the end of Fish Row is a medieval timber-framed house, mistakenly associated with – and named after – one of the city's wealthy wool merchants, John a'Port. Although much altered inside, architectural riches are still to be found, including fine 17th-century oak panelling, and a stone fireplace with carved chimneypiece. Today, the building is occupied by a glass and china shop, and a ghost named Oliver.

THE WHITE HART

Standing majestically on St John's Street is the White Hart Hotel, crested by a statue of the namesake of both the hotel and the chequer. On the day following a general election, the local Member of Parliament emerges onto the balcony of the Ionic portico, and gives voice to a song entitled 'The Fly on the Turnip'. One should perhaps be grateful that this event occurs only periodically!

John a Port's House

The White Hart

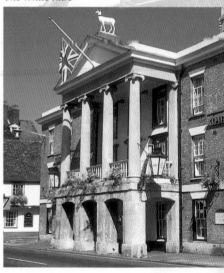

THE RED LION

The Red Lion, in Antelope Chequer, is part 14th-century, when it was a hostel for cathedral workmen. With the dawning of the coaching era it was extended, and for a while its galleried courtyard bustled each evening with the departure of the Salisbury Flying Machine for London. The lovely creeper that festoons the building is over a hundred years old.

THE PHEASANT

On the corner of Rollestone Street and Salt Lane, in Gore's Chequer, is an inn dating from the 15th century. In 1638 the house was bequeathed by the owner, Philip Crew, a schoolmaster, to the Shoemakers' Company, who built their guildhall alongside.

The courtyard of the Red Lion

The Pheasant Inn and Shoemakers' Hall

Around The Rows

Between the market place and New Canal are the 'Rows', enticingly named to reflect the business of those who traded there – Fish Row, Butcher Row, Ox Row, Oatmeal Row. In this quarter, too, were the four medieval market crosses, of which only one, the Poultry Cross, remains today. The others – the Cheese Cross, the Barnard's Cross and the Wool Cross – have long since disappeared.

THE POULTRY CROSS

A poultry cross has stood on the corner of Minster Street and Butcher Row since 1335. The lower section of the cross seen today dates from the end of the 15th century; this plain but workmanlike structure was embellished in Victorian times by ornate flying buttresses surrounding a central pinnacle.

ST THOMAS'S CHURCH

The first St Thomas's Church was a wooden chapel, built for labourers working on the cathedral, and is truly the townspeople's church. After 1450 it was rebuilt in stone, in Perpendicular Gothic style. The marvellous Doom painting over the chancel arch dates from 1475, but was whitewashed over and remained so for 300 years. It was uncovered in 1881 to show the good ascending from their graves on the left, and the evil descending to hell on the right. Recently, one bay of the angel ceiling has been restored, revealing the rich medieval colours.

Snell's Tea Rooms

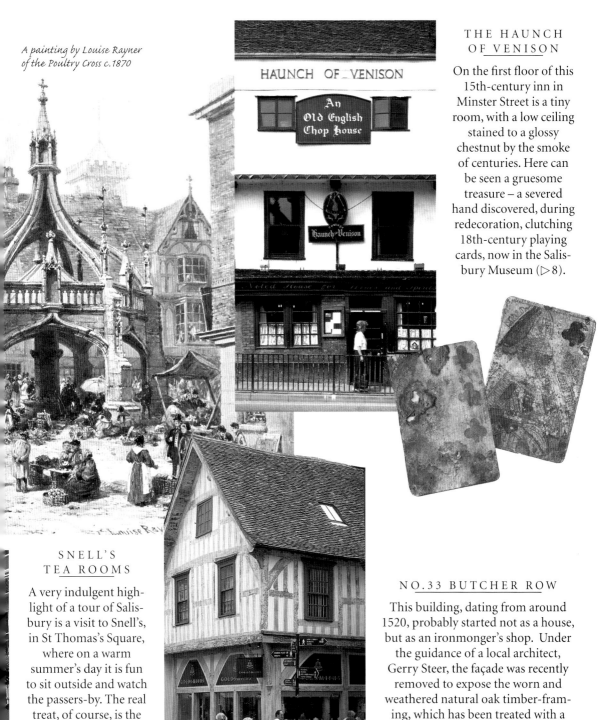

A painting by Louise Rayner of the Poultry Cross c.1870

HAUNCH OF VENISON

An Old English Chop house

THE HAUNCH OF VENISON

On the first floor of this 15th-century inn in Minster Street is a tiny room, with a low ceiling stained to a glossy chestnut by the smoke of centuries. Here can be seen a gruesome treasure – a severed hand discovered, during redecoration, clutching 18th-century playing cards, now in the Salisbury Museum (▷8).

SNELL'S TEA ROOMS

A very indulgent highlight of a tour of Salisbury is a visit to Snell's, in St Thomas's Square, where on a warm summer's day it is fun to sit outside and watch the passers-by. The real treat, of course, is the mouth-watering selection of cakes and pastries to be enjoyed with a refreshing drink.

NO.33 BUTCHER ROW

This building, dating from around 1520, probably started not as a house, but as an ironmonger's shop. Under the guidance of a local architect, Gerry Steer, the façade was recently removed to expose the worn and weathered natural oak timber-framing, which has been treated with a lime-wash instead of the dark stain used more often.

No.33 Butcher Row

Out of Town Visits

Within a few miles of Salisbury there are ancient stone circles, historic houses and restful gardens to be explored, as well as the beautiful and atmospheric Wiltshire countryside.

STONEHENGE

Mystery surrounds the origins of this strange, prehistoric stone circle. How were the huge stones transported, some from as far away as the Prescelly Mountains in South Wales – and why? Who was responsible for a construction so solid that much of it still stands after 4,000 years? Who gathered here to greet the midsummer sunrise, and what rituals were performed? A visit to this World Heritage Site, of such importance that it can now only be marvelled at from a respectful distance, is not to be missed.

WILTON HOUSE

A fine art collection and magnificent antiques are to be found in this stately and elegant Palladian house, designed by Inigo Jones and home of the Earls of Pembroke. For younger visitors, there is the miniature splendour of the Pembroke Palace Dolls' House, a gathering of costumed teddies known as the Wareham Bears, and a playground that is truly adventurous. A stroll around the tranquil landscaped parkland, alongside the River Nadder, is a joy in itself.

HEALE GARDEN

Open all year round, Heale Garden, in its eight-acre setting alongside the River Avon, is beautiful throughout the seasons. Early spring flowers and magnolias give way to roses at the height of summer, followed by the splendid autumn colour of acers in the water garden.

BREAMORE HOUSE

Nine miles south of Salisbury is Breamore, a 16th-century manor house with collections of paintings, needlework, furniture and porcelain. In the grounds visitors can get a taste of country life in the 17th century – full-sized replicas include a farm-worker's cottage, a blacksmith's shop and a dairy.

WILTON CARPET FACTORY

The famous 'Wilton weave' carpet was invented in the 18th century, and, although the traditional hand loom has given way to the power loom, it is fascinating to tour the modern factory and see the carpets in production. The history of carpet-making is demonstrated in the factory museum.

FARMER GILES WORKING FARM

Children can experience 'hands-on' farming on this working dairy farm – bottle-feeding lambs, grooming donkeys and hand-milking the Jersey cow are only a few of the educational but fun activities on offer here.

MUSEUM OF ARMY FLYING AND EXPLORERS' WORLD

The history of Army flying from before the Great War to the present day is displayed at the Middle Wallop Airfield. Explorers' World, an interactive science and education centre, appeals to children of all ages.

CHOLDERTON RARE BREEDS FARM PARK

Rare and endangered breeds of farm animals are lovingly nurtured here, and children can enjoy close contact with many of them – rabbits, goats and piglets. There are water gardens, an adventure playground and a nature trail, but the highlight of the visit may well be the 'Pork Stakes' pig race!

City Plan

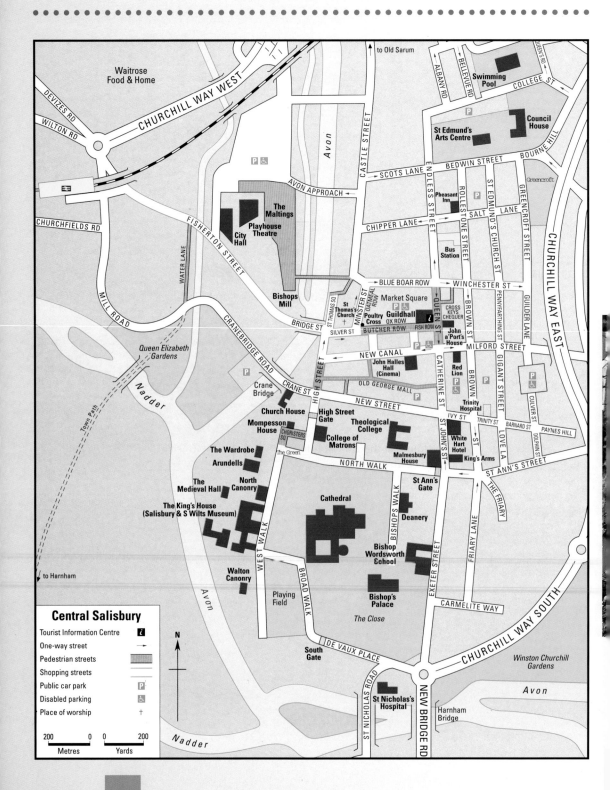

Central Salisbury

Tourist Information Centre	_i_
One-way street	→
Pedestrian streets	
Shopping streets	
Public car park	P
Disabled parking	♿
Place of worship	†

200 0 0 200
Metres   Yards

Waitrose Food & Home
to Old Sarum
CHURCHILL WAY WEST
DEVIZES RD
WILTON RD
CHURCHFIELDS RD
MILL ROAD
FISHERTON STREET
WATER LANE
Avon
Castle Street
Swimming Pool
ALBANY RD
BELLEVUE RD
QUEEN'S RD
COLLEGE ST
Council House
St Edmund's Arts Centre
BOURNE HILL
SCOTS LANE
BEDWIN STREET
Greencroft
ENDLESS STREET
ROLLESTONE STREET
SALT LANE
ST EDMUND'S CHURCH ST
GREENCROFT STREET
CHURCHILL WAY EAST
Pheasant Inn
CHIPPER LANE
AVON APPROACH
The Maltings
Playhouse Theatre
City Hall
Bus Station
BLUE BOAR ROW
WINCHESTER ST
ST THOMAS SQ
MINSTER ST
OATMEAL ROW
Market Square
Guildhall
OX ROW
CROSS KEYS CHEQUER
Queen St
BROWN ST
PENNYFARTHING ST
GUILDER LANE
Bishops Mill
St Thomas' Church
Poultry Cross
SILVER ST
BUTCHER ROW
FISH ROW
John a'Port's House
MILFORD STREET
GIGANT STREET
CULVER ST
BRIDGE ST
CRANEBRIDGE ROAD
Queen Elizabeth Gardens
Nadder
Town Path
HIGH STREET
NEW CANAL
John Halles Hall (Cinema)
OLD GEORGE MALL
Red Lion
CATHERINE ST
Trinity Hospital
CRANE ST
Crane Bridge
NEW STREET
IVY ST
ST JOHN'S ST
TRINITY ST
BARNARD ST
PAYNES HILL
DOLPHIN ST
Church House
High Street Gate
Theological College
Mompesson House
CHORISTERS SQ
The Green
College of Matrons
Malmesbury House
White Hart Hotel
King's Arms
LOVE LA
The Wardrobe
Arundells
NORTH WALK
St Ann's Gate
ST ANN'S STREET
THE FRIARY
The Medieval Hall
North Canonry
BISHOPS WALK
Deanery
The King's House (Salisbury & S Wilts Museum)
Cathedral
Bishop Wordsworth School
FRIARY LANE
to Harnham
Walton Canonry
WEST WALK
BROAD WALK
Playing Field
The Close
Bishop's Palace
EXETER STREET
CARMELITE WAY
CHURCHILL WAY SOUTH
Winston Churchill Gardens
Avon
DE VAUX PLACE
South Gate
ST NICHOLAS ROAD
NEW BRIDGE RD
St Nicholas's Hospital
Harnham Bridge
Nadder
Avon
to Harnham

N

32